Copyright © 2024 Jack Zhang

All rights reserved

The content of this book, including but not limited to the strategies, information, and examples provided in various chapters, is intended for general guidance only and does not constitute legal, financial, professional, or any other form of specific advice. The narratives and examples are based on real-life events and personal accounts; however, they should be viewed as illustrative rather than prescriptive. Individual results can vary, and success in business often requires hard work, good timing, and occasionally, a bit of luck. Readers should consider their unique circumstances and are strongly advised to seek personalized advice from qualified professionals in legal, financial, tax, business development, customer relationship management, and technology fields to address their specific needs. The regulatory environments, technological solutions, and business strategies discussed are general suggestions and may need to be adapted to fit specific operational needs, financial capabilities, and local dynamics. The author and publisher disclaim any liability for any loss or damage that may arise from reliance on, or use of, the information contained in this book.

No part of this book may be reproduced, or stored in a retrieval system, or transmitted in any form or by any means, electronic, mechanical, photocopying, recording, or otherwise, without express written permission of the publisher.

ISBN: 9798325338793

Cover design by: Jack Zhang

CONTENTS

Copyright	
Introduction	
Chapter 1: The Entrepreneurial Spirit	1
Chapter 2: Common Pitfalls and How to Avoid Them	5
Chapter 3: Financial Management	9
Chapter 4: Customer Relations	13
Chapter 5: Technology and Innovation	17
Chapter 6: Scaling and Growth	21
Chapter 7: The Role of Community	25
Chapter 8: Navigating Regulations	28
Final Chapter: Charting Your Path Forward	32
Appendix - Checklist for Starting and Running a Small Business	35
Afterword	37
About The Author	39

INTRODUCTION

A Casual Conversation that Sparked a Mission

It all began over a simple cup of coffee—a casual chat with a local café owner in Sydney that turned into a transformative 30-minute conversation. As she crafted my order, our light-hearted exchange evolved into an enlightening discussion about business operations, challenges, and strategies. By the end of our chat, not only did I leave with a freshly brewed coffee, but I also gained a profound realisation: much of the essential knowledge and practices crucial for running a successful small business were either neglected, overlooked, or closely guarded by hardworking owners caught up in their daily routines.

This revelation was not just a moment of insight but a call to action. It propelled me to harness my decade of experience in institutional finance and my extensive interactions with small business owners—from cafés to legal practices—to create a guide that could potentially enlighten and empower even just one entrepreneur. This book, "Thriving Down Under: Lessons from Australia's Frontline Small Businesses," is the culmination of that mission. It is designed to arm small business owners with the knowledge and strategies they need to not only survive but thrive, especially during challenging economic times.

From International Property To Local Business Insight

My journey into the world of small businesses wasn't

straightforward. It began in the realm of international property investment, where I brokered deals that brought Chinese investors to Australian shores. This role expanded significantly in 2015 when I partnered with an international investment consultancy based in China, diving deeper into the complexities of property markets and development projects.

Significant turning points came with my involvement in development projects in locations like Gosford and The Entrance, eventually leading to a key role as Project Manager and Director for a prime residential development in Sydney's Bellevue Hill. However, the project stumbled over multiple hurdles and ultimately did not proceed as planned. This setback was a critical learning point for me, pushing me to pursue formal education in property to systematically refine my understanding and skills.

Today, as a Registered Valuer servicing a wide array of asset classes nationwide, I have carved out a niche in interviewing and understanding the needs and challenges of small business owners. My professional evolution has equipped me with a unique perspective on the nexus between property management and small business operations, particularly in how external factors like location and economic climate can drastically impact business success.

Observations In A Post-Pandemic World

The COVID-19 pandemic has undeniably reshaped the landscape of small businesses in Australia. Since 2020, one of the most vocal concerns I've heard from business owners relates to the skyrocketing costs of rent and the stringent conditions of rental agreements post-pandemic. Many have found themselves grappling with the dual challenges of fulfilling rental obligations and sustaining adequate customer traffic, especially as some streets remain sparsely populated, echoing the economic and social repercussions of the pandemic.

These insights are not just passing observations but are pivotal to understanding the resilience and adaptability of businesses in times of crisis. They underscore the necessity for entrepreneurs to be equipped with not only the knowledge to navigate through such challenges but also the foresight to anticipate and mitigate potential risks.

The Objective: Empowerment Through Knowledge

This book aims to dissect these complexities and offer tangible, practical advice. The goal is to address the proverbial elephant in the room—how to sustain and grow a business during economic downturns. By highlighting the skillsets most valued by professionals and seasoned business owners, this guide seeks to remind readers of the crucial knowledge and mindset shifts required to transition from worker to successful businessperson.

Moreover, it aims to inspire and equip the next generation of entrepreneurs, particularly young adults eager to embark on their own business ventures. The lessons and strategies outlined in this book are intended to serve as both a beacon and a toolkit for navigating the tumultuous waters of business ownership.

Overview Of What Lies Ahead

In the chapters that follow, we will delve into the Entrepreneurial Spirit, uncovering the drive and determination that fuel successful enterprises. We will explore Common Pitfalls and how to sidestep them, manage Finances effectively, and cultivate strong Customer Relations. We'll discuss the pivotal role of Technology and Innovation in modern business, strategies for Scaling and Growth, the importance of Community engagement, and the intricacies of Navigating Regulations.

Each chapter is designed to build on the one before, creating a comprehensive roadmap for current and aspiring small business owners across Australia. With practical advice, real-world examples, and actionable strategies, "Thriving Down Under" aims to equip you with the knowledge to not just navigate but excel in the world of small business.

Disclaimer: Legal And Professional Advice

Please note that while this book provides general guidance and insights into managing a small business, it does not constitute legal, financial, or professional advice. Specific circumstances vary greatly, and as such, readers should seek personalised advice from qualified professionals in legal, financial, tax, and business fields to address their unique needs.

CHAPTER 1: THE ENTREPRENEURIAL SPIRIT

Understanding the Entrepreneurial Mindset

At the core of every successful business venture lies the entrepreneurial spirit—a unique blend of vision, resilience, passion, and adaptability. This chapter explores what it means to embody this spirit through the stories of three individuals whose journeys underscore the essence of entrepreneurship.

David Fogarty's Journey From Insecurity To Financial Freedom

Background: David Fogarty's story is not just about financial success; it's about personal transformation. Once a struggling student in Adelaide, plagued by insecurity and academic challenges, David's life took a turn following a stern ultimatum from his parents to work harder or face serious consequences.

Turning Point: The catalyst for David's change was his exposure to motivational content, including inspirational Nike commercials emphasizing the value of hard work and embracing failure. He adopted small but significant habits, such as regular gym visits and tutoring, which not only improved his grades but also built his confidence.

Entrepreneurial Venture: David initially made his mark through an Instagram business that evolved into a platform for advertising fitness brands, eventually earning six figures. Despite setbacks, including a failed food franchise and a costly scam, his determination led him to success in e-commerce.

Key Takeaways:

Embrace small, consistent efforts; they compound over time and lead to significant life improvements.

Persistence and the willingness to learn from failures are crucial for overcoming setbacks and achieving success.

Scott & Mina O'neill's Property Empire

Background: Scott and Mina O'Neill started their journey in 2010 with a modest approach to property investment. Initially performing renovations themselves, they quickly realised the potential for scaling their efforts.

Business Growth: Their hands-on strategy expanded into a 20-property portfolio. The couple now runs Rethink Investing, a buyer's agency that has grown to offer services in property insurance, legal advice, and renewable energy, employing 50 people.

Living the Dream: The O'Neills' success allows them to spend half the year in their house in Greece, showcasing the lifestyle freedom that successful entrepreneurship can provide.

Key Takeaways:

Hands-on involvement and a deep understanding of your industry are crucial in the early stages of your business.

Diversification within your niche can lead to business growth and personal freedom.

Werner Liu's Quiet Revolution In E-Commerce

Background: Werner Liu began with a simple business model—buying items from dollar shops and selling them for a profit on eBay. This humble beginning set the stage for what would become one of Australia's largest dropshipping operations.

Business Evolution: Liu's company, New Aim, grew to fill the online stores of hundreds of sellers, including giants like Amazon and Temple & Webster. Despite a business vision clash that led to his buyout in 2021, Liu's strategies and innovations remain influential in the e-commerce space.

Financial Outcome: Liu's entrepreneurial spirit and savvy business practices led to a substantial $101 million cash payout from his business partner, showcasing the potential financial rewards of innovative business models.

Key Takeaways:

Start small and scale gradually; the digital landscape offers vast opportunities for growth.

A clear vision and innovative strategies are essential for staying ahead in competitive industries.

Cultivating Your Entrepreneurial Spirit

This chapter showcases the diverse paths to success and underscores the universal traits that define the entrepreneurial spirit. Whether it's turning personal struggles into motivational success stories, like David Fogarty, innovating within traditional industries like the O'Neills, or revolutionising retail through e-commerce like Werner Liu, these entrepreneurs exemplify the drive and adaptability necessary to succeed. For emerging business owners, these stories provide both inspiration and practical lessons on embodying the entrepreneurial spirit in their ventures.

Disclaimer: Personal And Business Growth

The stories featured in this chapter are based on real-life events and personal accounts. However, they should be viewed as examples rather than prescriptions. Individual results may vary, and success in business requires a combination of hard work, timing, and sometimes, a bit of luck. Always consider your unique circumstances and seek advice tailored to your situation.

CHAPTER 2: COMMON PITFALLS AND HOW TO AVOID THEM

In the journey of entrepreneurship, the road to success is often paved with challenges that can either forge a path to success or lead to setbacks. Understanding these common pitfalls and learning how to navigate around them is crucial for any business owner. This chapter explores several frequent challenges that entrepreneurs face and offers practical advice on how to avoid them.

Pitfall 1: Insufficient Market Research

Problem: Many businesses fail because they don't adequately understand their market. Entrepreneurs often assume there's a demand for their product or service without thorough research to back up those assumptions.

Solution: Conduct extensive market research before launching your business. This should include identifying your target demographic, understanding their needs and preferences, and analysing competitors. Tools such as surveys, focus groups, and market analysis reports can provide valuable insights.

Pitfall 2: Poor Financial Management

Problem: Mismanagement of finances is one of the leading reasons small businesses fail. This includes everything from insufficient initial funding to poor handling of cash flows and expenses.

Solution: Develop a robust financial plan that includes detailed budgets, forecasts, and contingencies. It's often beneficial to consult with a financial advisor or employ accounting software to keep track of your finances meticulously.

Pitfall 3: Ignoring Customer Feedback

Problem: Businesses that fail to listen to their customers can miss out on crucial feedback that could improve their product or service.

Solution: Implement systems to regularly collect, analyze, and act on customer feedback. Whether through online reviews, social media, or direct customer surveys, understanding what your customers want is key to continuous improvement and satisfaction.

Pitfall 4: Underestimating The Importance Of Marketing

Problem: Many entrepreneurs believe that a good product or service will sell itself. However, without effective marketing, even the best offerings can fail to reach potential customers.

Solution: Develop a comprehensive marketing strategy that utilises both digital and traditional marketing channels. Tailor your approach to meet the needs and habits of your target audience. Investing in good marketing can significantly enhance your visibility and sales.

Pitfall 5: Lack Of Adaptability

Problem: The market is always changing, and businesses that fail to adapt can quickly become obsolete. This includes failing to update products, ignoring new consumer trends, or sticking rigidly to an outdated business model.

Solution: Stay flexible and be willing to pivot your strategy as necessary. Keep an eye on industry trends and be ready to make changes to your business model, products, or services as your market evolves.

Pitfall 6: Neglecting Legal And Regulatory Requirements

Problem: Small businesses can face significant risks if they fail to comply with legal and regulatory requirements. This could include fines, lawsuits, or serious business disruptions.

Solution: Ensure that you understand the legal and regulatory landscape of your industry. This may involve consulting with legal experts, staying updated on changes in regulations, and maintaining necessary licenses and permits.

Pitfall 7: Ineffective Leadership And Management

Problem: Poor management can demotivate employees, lead to inefficiency, and ultimately harm business operations. This often stems from a lack of clear direction, poor communication, or inadequate leadership skills.

Solution: Invest in developing strong leadership skills and management practices. This includes clear communication, setting clear goals and expectations, and fostering a positive and productive work environment.

Pitfall 8: Overexpansion

Problem: Expanding too quickly can stretch resources thin and lead to quality control, financial, or operational issues.

Solution: Focus on growing your business sustainably. Ensure that each step of expansion is well-planned and adequately funded, and that you have the operational capacity to manage growth without compromising on the quality of your products or services.

Conclusion: Staying Vigilant And Proactive

Avoiding these common pitfalls doesn't just require awareness but also proactive planning and execution. By understanding the typical challenges faced by small businesses and adopting strategies to mitigate them, entrepreneurs can not only avoid common pitfalls but also position their businesses for long-term success and stability. This chapter aims to provide you with the knowledge and tools necessary to navigate the complex landscape of entrepreneurship with confidence.

Disclaimer: Legal And Professional Advice

Please note that while this book provides general guidance on managing common business challenges, it does not constitute legal, financial, or professional advice. Specific circumstances vary greatly, and as such, readers should seek personalised advice from qualified professionals in legal, financial, tax, and business fields to address their unique needs.

CHAPTER 3: FINANCIAL MANAGEMENT

Effective financial management is crucial for the success and sustainability of any small business. Understanding the basics of financial operations and implementing sound strategies can significantly increase the likelihood of a business thriving in the long term. This chapter delves into essential financial knowledge for small business owners and presents real-life case studies that demonstrate effective financial strategies in action.

Essential Financial Knowledge For Small Businesses

Understanding Financial Statements: The backbone of sound financial management lies in the ability to understand and utilise financial statements. Three key statements every entrepreneur should be familiar with are the balance sheet, income statement, and cash flow statement. These documents provide a comprehensive overview of your business's financial health, showing where money comes from, where it goes, and how it is allocated.

Budgeting and Forecasting: Effective budgeting is crucial for planning and controlling your financial resources. A detailed budget helps you forecast future revenue and expenses, align your business goals with financial reality, and manage cash flow effectively. Regularly comparing actual results with your budget can highlight variances and prompt necessary adjustments.

Cash Flow Management: Cash flow is the lifeblood of any

business. Managing cash flow involves tracking the timing and amount of cash inflows and outflows. Techniques for improving cash flow include speeding up receivables, managing payables wisely, and keeping reserves for unexpected challenges.

Cost Management and Reduction: Identifying and controlling unnecessary costs can make a significant difference in your profitability. Regularly review your expenses and assess whether each cost is justified and contributes to your business objectives. Consider alternative suppliers or less expensive solutions that do not compromise quality or customer satisfaction.

Debt Management: While debt can be a powerful tool for growth, mismanaged debt is one of the quickest ways for a business to become unsustainable. Understand the terms of any loans, including interest rates and repayment schedules, and ensure that your business can comfortably meet these obligations without compromising its operational capacity.

Understanding Taxes and Benefits: Taxes can significantly affect your business's bottom line. Stay informed about tax obligations and potential benefits, such as deductions and credits. Proper tax planning with a professional can help minimise liabilities and boost profitability.

Ase Studies On Effective Financial Strategies

Case Study 1: Tech Start-Up Scaling Smartly

A Melbourne-based tech start-up initially struggled with cash flow management during its growth phase. The founders implemented a strict budgeting and forecasting system that allowed them to plan for major expenditures and manage day-to-day expenses more effectively. They also secured a line of credit with favourable terms that provided the necessary cash flow to support growth without the pressure of immediate repayments. This strategic financial planning supported a smooth scaling process and helped the start-up establish a strong market

position.
Key Takeaways:
Implement robust budgeting and forecasting to manage finances during expansion.
Secure financing with manageable terms to support growth without overleveraging.

Case Study 2: Retail Store Maximizing Profit Margins

A small retail store in Sydney implemented a cost-reduction strategy by renegotiating supplier contracts and optimising inventory levels to reduce holding costs. The owners also introduced an automated inventory management system that minimised overstocking and understocking issues, thereby enhancing cash flow and reducing unnecessary expenditures. These strategic moves not only lowered costs but also improved overall efficiency, leading to higher profit margins.
Key Takeaways:
Regularly review and renegotiate supplier contracts to reduce costs.
Invest in technology that improves operational efficiency and financial health.

Case Study 3: Café Chain Utilizing Tax Benefits

The owner of a chain of cafes in Perth made significant savings by consulting with a tax advisor to understand all applicable deductions, including those for small businesses. The advisor helped the café chain restructure some of its financial practices to maximise these benefits. They also implemented energy-saving measures that qualified for green energy tax credits, reducing their tax liabilities and operational costs simultaneously.
Key Takeaways:
Consult with tax professionals to ensure you are taking full advantage of all applicable tax benefits.

Consider investments that not only save money but may also provide tax benefits.

Conclusion: Building A Financially Sound Business

Mastering financial management involves a combination of understanding fundamental financial principles, applying these in a disciplined way, and always seeking ways to optimise financial operations. By learning from the experiences of other businesses, as illustrated in the case studies, and applying these lessons, small business owners can build more financially stable and successful enterprises. This chapter provides the knowledge and tools to navigate the complex financial landscapes that businesses face, aiming to secure a prosperous future.

Disclaimer: Financial And Tax Advice

This chapter provides general financial and tax information and is not intended to be a substitute for professional advice. Readers are advised to consult qualified financial advisors or tax professionals to obtain advice tailored to their specific circumstances.

CHAPTER 4: CUSTOMER RELATIONS

Good customer relations are the lifeblood of any successful business. This chapter explores the critical role of customer service and retention in sustaining and growing a business. It delves into effective strategies and real-world examples of excellent customer service practices that have proven successful for businesses.

The Importance Of Customer Service And Retention

Customer Loyalty: At the heart of customer relations is the creation of loyalty. Loyal customers not only repeat purchases but also become advocates for your brand, promoting it through word-of-mouth. Research shows that increasing customer retention by just 5% can boost profits by 25% to 95%.

Customer Feedback: Effective customer service transforms feedback into actionable insights. Listening to customers helps businesses adapt and improve their offerings, ensuring that the services or products remain relevant and desirable.

Brand Reputation: In the digital age, a company's reputation can be significantly influenced by its customer service. Positive customer experiences often lead to beneficial reviews online, which enhance the brand's public image and attract new customers.

Real Examples Of Excellent Customer Service Practices

Case Study 1: Zappos' Customer-Centric Approach

Background: Zappos, an online shoe and clothing retailer, has become synonymous with exceptional customer service. Their philosophy is to "deliver WOW through service."
Strategies:
24/7 Customer Support: Zappos offers around-the-clock customer service, ensuring that customer queries are never left unanswered for long.
365-Day Return Policy: Their very generous return policy removes the risk of online shopping, encouraging purchases.
Empowering Employees: Zappos employees are trained and empowered to go above and beyond to satisfy customers, including sending flowers or free products to dissatisfied customers.
Outcome:
These practices have not only earned Zappos a loyal customer base but also a stellar reputation in the retail industry, translating into substantial business growth.

Case Study 2: The Ritz-Carlton's Empowered Service Model

Background: The Ritz-Carlton hotel chain is renowned for its luxurious service standards and personalised customer care.
Strategies:
Employee Empowerment: Every employee is empowered to spend up to $2,000 (per incident) to solve any guest's problem without needing further approval.
Personalised Guest Experiences: Staff members are encouraged to personalise guest experiences and anticipate needs, often using

previous stay data to enhance comfort.

Outcome:

This approach has consistently placed The Ritz-Carlton at the top of customer satisfaction indices in the hospitality industry.

Case Study 3: Amazon's Focus on Convenience

Background: Amazon has revolutionised the retail sector with its focus on customer service, particularly through convenience and innovation.

Strategies:

User-Friendly Interfaces: Amazon's platforms are designed with the user experience in mind, making browsing and purchasing straightforward.

Prime Membership: Offers benefits like free two-day shipping, streaming services, and exclusive deals, creating a high-value proposition for customers.

Efficient Problem Resolution: Amazon has a robust system for handling customer complaints and issues, often prioritising customer satisfaction in disputes.

Outcome:

Amazon's customer-centric strategies have made it one of the most valuable companies in the world, with a vast and loyal customer base.

Strategies For Effective Customer Service And Retention

Training and Development: Regular training programs for employees can ensure that they remain skilled in customer service practices. Role-playing customer scenarios and discussing real cases can prepare them to handle various situations.

Technology and Automation: Utilizing CRM (Customer Relationship Management) systems can help track customer interactions, preferences, and history. Automated services like chatbots can provide immediate assistance to customers, improving their experience.

Feedback Loops: Implementing systematic feedback collection

and analysis can help businesses understand customer needs and dissatisfaction points. This feedback should be regularly reviewed and used to make necessary adjustments to products or services.

Loyalty Programs: Developing loyalty programs that reward repeat customers can significantly enhance retention rates. These programs should offer genuine value to ensure they are attractive and effective.

Community Building: Creating a sense of community around a brand can lead to stronger emotional connections. Forums, social media groups, and regular customer events can foster this sense of belonging.

Conclusion

Excellent customer relations are not just about handling complaints and queries; they are about creating an overarching experience that makes customers feel valued and respected. By focusing on personalised service, consistent quality, and proactive customer engagement, businesses can build a loyal customer base that drives growth and profitability. This chapter provides actionable insights and examples that businesses can adapt to enhance their customer service practices and develop enduring relationships with their clients.

Disclaimer: General Advice

This chapter provides general customer service and relationship management strategies. While these strategies are broadly applicable, the effectiveness of specific approaches may vary based on individual business circumstances and industry contexts. Businesses should adapt the suggestions herein to their specific needs and consider consulting with customer relationship experts to optimise their strategies.

CHAPTER 5: TECHNOLOGY AND INNOVATION

In today's rapidly evolving marketplace, leveraging technology is not just an option for small businesses—it's essential for staying competitive and relevant. This chapter explores how technology can effectively enhance business operations, improve customer engagement, and drive growth. It also provides general advice tailored to common types of small businesses in Australia, such as cafes, bakeries, and mechanics.

Leveraging Technology In Small Businesses

Streamlining Operations: Technology can significantly enhance operational efficiency across various sectors. Automation of routine tasks like inventory management, appointment scheduling, and billing can free up time for strategic activities, reduce human error, and lead to cost savings.

Enhancing Customer Experience: Digital tools can help businesses offer more personalised and convenient customer experiences. Implementing a CRM (Customer Relationship Management) system, for example, can enable businesses to track customer interactions, analyse behaviour, and tailor marketing efforts to meet individual preferences and needs.

Expanding Market Reach: Utilizing online platforms, social media, and e-commerce websites can dramatically extend a business's reach beyond local boundaries. These tools allow small businesses to tap into new markets and demographics at a fraction of the cost of traditional marketing methods.

Improving Data Security: With the increasing risk of cyber threats, investing in robust security software and adhering to best practices in IT security is crucial for protecting sensitive business and customer data.

General Advice For Common Business Types

Cafes and Bakeries:

Point of Sale (POS) Systems: Modern POS systems can integrate sales, inventory, and customer management, providing valuable insights into business performance and customer preferences, which can help in making informed decisions.

Online Ordering Systems: Implementing an online ordering system can streamline operations, reduce wait times, and improve customer satisfaction. It can also expand sales opportunities beyond the traditional walk-in business model.

Mechanics and Auto Repair Shops:

Booking and Scheduling Software: Use digital tools to manage bookings and schedule repairs. This technology can help reduce double bookings, manage customer expectations, and optimise workflow.

Digital Vehicle Inspection Tools: These tools can provide customers with digital reports that detail the condition of their vehicles. Such transparency can increase trust and customer satisfaction.

General Small Retailers:

E-commerce Platforms: Setting up an online store can complement physical retail operations, allowing businesses to reach a broader audience. Platforms like Shopify or WooCommerce can be integrated with minimal hassle to manage both online and in-store sales.

Inventory Management Software: Automate inventory tracking to reduce the likelihood of overstocking or stockouts, which can tie up capital and affect sales. Advanced systems can predict inventory needs based on sales trends.

Harnessing Technology for Growth

Investing in the Right Tools: It's crucial for businesses to select technologies that align with their specific operational needs and growth goals. Return on investment should always be a key consideration.

Training and Adaptation: To get the most out of new technologies, businesses must invest in training their staff. Proper understanding and usage of technology are essential for maximising its benefits.

Staying Updated on Trends: Technology is continually evolving, and so are the needs and expectations of customers. Businesses must stay informed about the latest technological advancements and industry trends to remain competitive.

Conclusion

For small businesses in today's digital age, embracing technology and innovation is essential for success. Whether it's a café looking to implement a new POS system, a mechanic shop adopting digital inspection tools, or a small bakery exploring online sales options, technology can drive significant improvements in efficiency, customer satisfaction, and business growth. This chapter provides a roadmap for small business owners to assess their technology needs and integrate solutions that will best support their business objectives.

Disclaimer: Technology Implementation

The technological solutions discussed in this chapter are general suggestions and should be considered starting points. Businesses should conduct detailed analyses to determine which technologies will best meet their specific operational needs and financial capabilities. Consultation with technology experts is recommended to tailor solutions that fit precise business requirements and budgets.

CHAPTER 6: SCALING AND GROWTH

Scaling a business is a pivotal stage in the entrepreneurial journey. It involves expanding operations effectively to meet increasing market demand without compromising the quality or performance of the business. This chapter discusses when and how to scale your business and features stories of businesses that have successfully navigated this challenging phase.

When To Scale Your Business

Clear Market Demand: Consider scaling when there's a consistent increase in demand for your products or services, indicating that the market can sustain growth.

Solid Infrastructure: Before scaling, ensure that foundational aspects of your business, such as supply chains, staffing, and systems, are robust enough to handle expansion without breaking down.

Financial Health: Scaling often requires significant investment. Ensure your business is financially stable, with enough cash flow to cover scaling costs and sustain operations during the expansion phase.

Strategic Planning: Have a clear strategy for scaling, including target markets, growth milestones, and an operational roadmap that aligns with your business goals.

How To Scale Your Business

Enhancing Operational Efficiency: Streamline processes through automation, outsourcing, or adopting new technologies. This can increase your capacity and improve service delivery without proportionally increasing costs.

Diversifying Products and Services: Explore opportunities to diversify your offerings to capture a broader market segment. This could involve introducing new products, variations of existing products, or complementary services.

Expanding to New Markets: Consider geographical expansion, either by entering new local markets or going international. Understand the new market's dynamics, culture, and consumer behaviour to tailor your offerings accordingly.

Building Strategic Partnerships: Form alliances with other businesses to leverage their resources, technology, or market presence. This can provide a shortcut to scale by accessing established networks and customer bases.

Acquiring Funding: Scaling may require additional funding. Options include reinvesting profits, seeking loans, attracting investors, or crowdfunding. Choose the best funding route based on your business's needs and risk tolerance.

Stories Of Successful Business Expansion

Case Study: Sydney-Based Mobile Carpet Cleaning Business

Background: Initially a weekend side project, this mobile carpet cleaning business was started by an individual in the Blue Mountains region of Sydney. The business idea took off rapidly after COVID-19, as residents, spending more time at home, became increasingly aware of the need for a clean environment.

Scaling Strategy:

Expanding Services: Observing that customers who needed carpet cleaning often also required lawn mowing services, the founder added lawn care to his offerings. This strategic decision allowed him to increase the value and appeal of his service.

Optimising Operations: To manage the growing workload and maximise efficiency, the founder employed his younger brother, training him in carpet cleaning to handle simpler jobs independently. This allowed the business to serve more customers simultaneously and reduce travel costs by offering multiple services in one visit.

Team Expansion: As demand continued to grow, the business expanded its workforce, hiring contractors and part-time employees. This not only increased operational capacity but also freed the founder to focus on business development and customer acquisition.

Outcome:

The strategic expansion and diversification of services quickly scaled the business across Western Sydney, significantly increasing its revenue and market presence. The efficient scaling strategy led to the successful sale of the mobile carpet cleaning division for over half a million dollars. The founder continues to operate in related verticals, including mobile car detailing and lawn mowing, leveraging the successful strategies and business model developed during the scaling of the carpet cleaning service.

Key Takeaways:

Leverage Related Services: Adding complementary services can significantly enhance business value and appeal to customers.

Strategic Employment: Employing and training family members or close associates as initial employees can be effective, especially when rapid scaling is needed.

Focus on Operational Efficiency: Optimizing how services are delivered can lead to significant cost savings and customer satisfaction improvements.

Capitalise on Expansion: Effective scaling can position a business as a lucrative acquisition target or allow it to expand into new related business areas.

Conclusion

Scaling a business is a delicate but essential step that requires careful planning and strategic execution. The stories provided illustrate various successful approaches to scaling, from product diversification and international expansion to adopting new business models like franchising. For entrepreneurs looking to expand, these stories offer valuable insights and strategies that can be adapted to their specific circumstances, ensuring that their growth is sustainable and profitable.

Disclaimer: Business Expansion Advice

The strategies discussed in this chapter are general and may not be applicable to all types of businesses or industries. Business owners should consider their unique situation and may benefit from consulting with business development experts to tailor a scaling strategy that best suits their needs.

CHAPTER 7: THE ROLE OF COMMUNITY

In business, particularly for small enterprises, the community plays a crucial role not just as a customer base but as a source of support, visibility, and growth. This chapter explores why building strong relationships within the community and with other businesses is essential and provides straightforward advice on overcoming common challenges faced by small businesses through community engagement.

The Importance Of Community Engagement

Mutual Support: In small business ecosystems, support from other local businesses can lead to shared resources, referrals, and collaborative marketing efforts, which are vital during both growth and downturns.

Enhancing Brand Loyalty: Companies active in their communities tend to enjoy deeper trust and loyalty from their customers. Community engagement shows that a business is interested in more than just profits—it's a part of the community fabric.

Gaining Local Insights: Engaging with the local community provides businesses with better insights into the needs and preferences of their customer base, allowing them to tailor products and services more effectively.

Strategies for Building Strong Community Relationships

Engage in Local Networks: Join local business associations, chambers of commerce, or networking groups. These organisations can provide valuable connections, resources, and local business insights that can mitigate common struggles like finding local suppliers or understanding regional market trends.

Participate in Community Events: Whether it's sponsoring a local sports team, participating in charity events, or setting up a booth at a local fair, involvement in community events raises your profile and shows your commitment to the community's welfare.

Collaborate Locally: Develop partnerships with nearby businesses to offer bundled services, co-host events, or support each other's marketing efforts. For example, a coffee shop and a bookstore might create a reading corner to attract more customers to both businesses.

Provide Community Support: Offering your expertise or resources to help local causes can establish your business as a reliable part of the community. This could be through mentoring local startups, providing internships to students, or offering your space for community meetings.

Utilise Local Media: Make use of local newspapers, radio stations, and community blogs for advertising and publicity. Local media often have strong community ties and can provide targeted exposure to your core demographic.

Common Small Business Struggles And Community Solutions

Struggle: Limited Marketing Budget

Solution: Leverage community bulletin boards, local events, and partnerships for low-cost marketing. Word-of-mouth can be powerful, so encourage satisfied customers to spread the word within the community.

Struggle: Building Customer Base

Solution: Offer community-specific promotions or loyalty programs. Engaging local influencers or community leaders can also be an effective way to attract a loyal customer base.

Struggle: Sourcing Local Talent

Solution: Connect with local educational institutions for internships or job fairs. Local networking groups can also be a good source of referrals for talented individuals looking for opportunities.

Struggle: Gaining Trust and Credibility

Solution: Consistently participate in and contribute to community activities. Trust builds over time, and consistent, positive community involvement can accelerate this process.

Struggle: Managing Business Growth

Solution: Seek advice and mentorship from established local business owners. Many communities have experienced entrepreneurs who are willing to share insights and strategies that can help you manage growth effectively.

Conclusion

Building strong community and business relationships is essential for small businesses. These connections can provide a network of support, enhance customer loyalty, and offer valuable local insights that can help overcome common business challenges. By actively engaging with the community, businesses not only contribute to their local economies but also establish a foundation for sustained growth and success.

Disclaimer: Community Engagement Advice

The strategies discussed in this chapter are general and should be adapted to the specific needs of your business and community. The effectiveness of these approaches can vary based on local dynamics and the specific characteristics of your business environment. Always consider consulting with local business advisors to tailor your community engagement strategies effectively.

CHAPTER 8: NAVIGATING REGULATIONS

Navigating the regulatory landscape is a critical aspect of managing a small business. Understanding and adhering to applicable laws and regulations can protect your business from legal issues and penalties while also ensuring ethical and compliant operations. This chapter explores the importance of understanding legal and regulatory hurdles, offers insights from business owners in highly regulated industries like liquor and law, and provides general cases to help small business owners recognise common regulatory challenges.

Understanding Legal And Regulatory Hurdles

Knowing Your Industry Regulations: Each industry has its own set of regulations. For example, food businesses must comply with health and safety standards, while technology companies may need to address privacy laws.

Local, State, and Federal Laws: Regulations can vary significantly across different levels of government. It's important for business owners to understand which regulations apply at the local, state, and federal levels.

Staying Updated: Laws and regulations can change frequently. Staying updated through reliable sources, industry associations, and legal advisories is crucial.

Insights From Regulated Industries

Liquor Industry Challenges: Business owners in the liquor industry often deal with complex licensing requirements, age verification laws, and restrictions on advertising. Regular training for staff on legal requirements and a strict compliance protocol can mitigate the risk of violations.

Legal Services Compliance: For those in the legal industry, maintaining client confidentiality and adhering to professional conduct standards are paramount. Implementing rigorous data security measures and ongoing professional development can help in staying compliant.

Common Regulatory Challenges And Solutions

Case Study 1: Meeting Health And Safety Standards

A small bakery is needed to ensure compliance with food safety regulations. The owner implemented a compliance program that included regular staff training, frequent health inspections, and a system for tracking food sources. This proactive approach not only helped to maintain high safety standards but also enhanced the bakery's reputation for quality.

Case Study 2: Navigating Employment Law

A retail store expanded quickly and needed to understand employment laws regarding wages, hours, and benefits. The owner consulted with a human resources (HR) professional to establish compliant employment practices and employee handbooks, which helped in avoiding potential legal issues and improving employee satisfaction.

Case Study 3: Adhering To Environmental Regulations

An auto repair shop faced challenges with waste disposal and environmental compliance. The owner worked with environmental consultants to implement eco-friendly waste disposal practices and ensure compliance with local environmental regulations, thus avoiding hefty fines and contributing to sustainability.

Strategies For Managing Regulatory Risks

Legal Consultation: Regular consultations with legal professionals can provide clarity and guidance on regulatory requirements and changes.

Compliance Training: Implementing a regular training program for all employees can help ensure that everyone understands and adheres to industry-specific regulations.

Risk Assessment: Conduct regular audits and risk assessments to identify potential compliance issues. Addressing these proactively can prevent legal problems and associated costs.

Joining Industry Associations: Membership in industry associations can provide access to resources, training, and updates on regulatory changes that affect your industry.

Technology Solutions: Utilize software and other technology tools designed to help businesses manage compliance and stay updated on regulations.

Conclusion

Understanding and navigating the regulatory environment is essential for the success and stability of any small business. While the challenges can be daunting, effectively managing legal and regulatory hurdles through proactive strategies and professional advice can significantly mitigate risks. Remember, the scenarios and advice provided in this chapter are for informational purposes and should not replace professional legal counsel. Always seek expert advice to ensure your business complies with applicable laws and regulations, thus safeguarding its future and reputation.

Disclaimer: Legal And Regulatory Advice

The information provided in this chapter is intended for general guidance only and does not constitute legal advice. Regulatory environments are complex and can vary widely by location and industry. It is crucial for business owners to consult with a qualified solicitor or legal advisor to obtain specific advice and ensure compliance with all applicable laws and regulations.

FINAL CHAPTER: CHARTING YOUR PATH FORWARD

As we close this guide, it's important to reflect on the journey we've undertaken together. Starting and running a small business is no small feat. It requires courage, resilience, and a continuous willingness to learn and adapt. Throughout this book, we've explored various facets of small business management—from cultivating the entrepreneurial spirit and managing finances effectively to leveraging technology, engaging with your community, and navigating the often complex legal landscape.

This final chapter is dedicated to synthesising these insights and setting a course for future growth and sustainability. Here, we'll summarise key takeaways, propose a strategy for ongoing learning, and discuss how to maintain the passion and perseverance needed to succeed in the dynamic world of small business.

Summarising Key Lessons

Each chapter of this book has provided critical insights and actionable advice designed to empower you, the small business owner, with the tools necessary to thrive:

Entrepreneurial Spirit: Remember the importance of passion, resilience, and vision in driving your business forward.

Financial Management: Keep a firm grasp on your finances, employing prudent budgeting, forecasting, and cash flow management.

Technology and Innovation: Stay abreast of technological advancements and think creatively to keep your business efficient and competitive.

Customer Relations: Prioritize customer satisfaction and loyalty, as these are the lifelines of your business's reputation and success.

Community Engagement: Build and nurture relationships within your community and industry for support, insight, and mutual growth.

Navigating Regulations: Understand and comply with the regulations affecting your business to avoid legal pitfalls and build a foundation of integrity.

Strategy for Ongoing Learning

The landscape of business is ever-changing, with new challenges and opportunities constantly arising. Commit to lifelong learning by:

Continuing Education: Engage in workshops, seminars, and courses that can enhance your business acumen.

Industry Participation: Join industry associations, attend trade shows, and subscribe to relevant publications to stay connected with trends and network with peers.

Feedback Loops: Regularly solicit feedback from customers, employees, and peers. This feedback is invaluable for continuous improvement.

Maintaining Passion And Perseverance

The journey of entrepreneurship is a marathon, not a sprint. Maintaining your initial passion and perseverance is crucial:

Work-Life Balance: Strive to maintain a balance that keeps you energised. Burnout is a common pitfall that can derail even the most passionate entrepreneurs.

Celebrate Milestones: Regularly reflect on and celebrate the achievements of your business. This not only motivates you but also your team.

Vision Adjustment: Be prepared to pivot or adjust your business vision based on market feedback and personal aspirations. Staying flexible can lead to unexpected and rewarding paths.

Conclusion

Your path as a small business owner is uniquely yours, yet it is also a journey shared by countless others who have navigated the triumphs and trials of entrepreneurship. As you move forward, take pride in the resilience you've shown thus far and the wisdom you've gained through each challenge faced.

Thank you for trusting this book as a guide along your path. Remember, the end of this book is just the beginning of your continued journey in mastering the art of small business. May your business not only survive but thrive in the changing tides of the economy, and may you find profound fulfilment in the work you do every day.

As we part ways in this literary form, let us part with a commitment to growth, not just in our businesses but in ourselves as leaders, innovators, and community members. Here's to your success today and in all the days to come.

APPENDIX - CHECKLIST FOR STARTING AND RUNNING A SMALL BUSINESS

Starting Up:

Business Plan: Develop a detailed business plan outlining your business idea, target market, value proposition, marketing & sales strategy, and financial projections.

Legal Structure: Decide on the legal structure of your business (e.g., sole trader, partnership, company) and register your business accordingly.

Business Name Registration: Register your business name with the Australian Securities and Investments Commission (ASIC).

Tax Registration: Obtain an Australian Business Number (ABN) and register for Goods and Services Tax (GST) if applicable.

Bank Account: Open a business bank account to separate personal and business finances.

Licenses and Permits: Identify and acquire any required local, state, or federal licenses and permits.

Insurance: Secure necessary insurance policies (e.g., public liability, professional indemnity, workers' compensation).

Running Your Business:

Accounting System: Set up an accounting system to manage your finances effectively (consider software like Xero, MYOB, or QuickBooks).
Budgeting: Establish a budget to monitor and control costs.
Inventory Management: Implement inventory management practices to optimise stock levels.
Customer Relationship Management (CRM): Adopt CRM tools to manage customer interactions and enhance customer service.
Marketing: Develop and execute ongoing marketing campaigns to attract and retain customers.
Compliance: Stay updated on legal and regulatory changes that affect your business.
Performance Review: Regularly review business performance against your goals and adjust your strategy as needed.

Growth And Expansion:

Market Research: Continuously research market trends and customer needs to identify new opportunities.
Innovation: Innovate your products or services to meet market demands and stay competitive.
Networking: Engage in networking to build relationships with other businesses and potential partners.
Employee Development: Invest in training and development for your employees.
Scalability: Plan and implement scalability strategies for your business operations.

AFTERWORD

A Message To Our Tenacious Readers

Congratulations on reaching the final page of "Thriving Down Under: Lessons from Australia's Frontline Small Businesses." If you've made it this far, it's clear you possess the dedication and drive essential for a successful entrepreneurial journey. You're not just preparing to navigate the complex world of small business—you are stepping up to master it.

Throughout this book, we've journeyed together through fundamental aspects of starting, managing, and growing a business in Australia. From igniting the entrepreneurial spirit to detailing strategies for financial management customer relations and navigating the often daunting regulatory landscape, we've covered a broad spectrum of essential topics. Each chapter was designed not only to inform but also to inspire and empower you to transform challenges into opportunities.

As you move forward, remember that the end of this book is not the conclusion of your learning. Let it be the beginning of an ongoing adventure in entrepreneurship. The path ahead will undoubtedly present challenges, but with the resilience and insights you've gained, these obstacles can become stepping stones to greater achievements.

We encourage you to keep this book close at hand as a reference as you continue to build and grow your business. Revisit the chapters as you encounter new situations or when you need a refresher on specific topics. Entrepreneurship is a dynamic journey—continual learning and adaptation are your best tools for sustained success.

Finally, share your journey with others. The experiences you gain and the lessons you learn can serve as invaluable advice for the next generation of entrepreneurs. Whether through mentoring, networking, or simply casual conversations like the one that sparked the creation of this book, your knowledge can inspire and elevate the entire small business community.

Thank you for trusting us to be a part of your entrepreneurial path. Here's to your success today and in all the days to come. May your business not only survive but thrive in the vibrant and ever-changing landscape of Australia's economy. Cheers to your future—a future built on perseverance, innovation, and the indomitable spirit that defines the very best of Australian small business owners.

With every good wish for your continued success,
Jack Zhang

ABOUT THE AUTHOR

Jack Zhang

About The Author
Jack is a seasoned entrepreneur and a trusted adviser in the world of small business. With over a decade of experience in institutional finance and property development, Jack has forged a career marked by resilience, innovation, and a deep commitment to community empowerment. A Registered Valuer and a former international property agent, he has an acute understanding of the Australian business landscape, which has been enriched by extensive interactions with small business owners across various industries—from cafés and bakeries to legal practices and tech startups. Jack's journey into entrepreneurship is a story of transformation and tenacity. After navigating several high-stakes development projects and experiencing both setbacks and successes, he found his true passion in helping other entrepreneurs achieve their business goals. Jack's approach combines practical advice with strategic insight, encouraging business owners to innovate, adapt, and thrive. Driven by the belief that small businesses are the backbone of the local economy, Jack authored "Thriving Down Under: Lessons from Australia's Frontline Small Businesses" to provide tools and wisdom to the next generation of entrepreneurs. When not consulting or writing, Jack enjoys exploring the great outdoors and actively participates in community initiatives that support local enterprises. Jack's pragmatic and personable writing style makes complex concepts accessible, turning the challenges of small business ownership into opportunities for growth. Through

his work, Jack aims to inspire and empower business owners to not just navigate but excel in Australia's dynamic economic landscape.

www.ingramcontent.com/pod-product-compliance
Lightning Source LLC
Chambersburg PA
CBHW050246230526
45470CB00005B/2139